First Lessons

Beginning Guitar: Learning Notes/Playing Solos

by William Bay

AUDIO CONTENTS

1	Introduction/How to Tune	31	#5	61	Salty Dog Blues
2	Tuning Notes	32	#6	62	Steal Away
3	E	33	#7	63	A String Notes
4	F	34	G-A	64	Study #2
5	G	35	Play 3 Strings	65	C Scale
6	E-F	36	German Song	66	Low Gear
7	F-G	37	Rock Feeling	67	Volga Boatmen
8	E-G	38	Indian Prayer	68	Power Drive
9	E-F-G	39	Good King Wenceslas	69	E String Notes
10	E-F-G (2 Notes Each)	40	African Hymn	70	#2
11	B	41	Rest Study	71	Note Review
12	C	42	I Know Where I Am Going	72	Angelina The Baker
13	D	43	8th Note Studies	73	The Water is Wide
14	B-C	44	Railroad Bill	74	F Sharp Studies
15	C-D	45	Rise and Shine	75	Can Can
16	B-D	46	#1	76	Polovetsian Dance
17	B-C-D	47	#2	77	Hey, Ho, Nobody's Home
18	B-C-D (2 Notes Each)	48	#3	78	I'm Gonna Play
19	#1	49	Downshift	79	Matty Groves
20	#2	50	What's Up?	80	Minuet by Bach
21	#3	51	Nascar	81	Waltzing Matilda
22	#4	52	Taps	82	Auld Lang Syne
23	#5	53	Reville	83	Finlandia Theme
24	#6	54	Lonesome Valley	84	B Flat Studies
25	#7	55	Our Boys Will Shine Tonight	85	Forest Green
26	#8	56	The Roving Gambler	86	Red Wing
27	#1	57	This Little Light of Mine	87	Once In David's Royal City
28	#2	58	Precious Memories	88	Waltz by Chopin
29	#3	59	Early American Hymn	89	Ding, Dong, Merrily on High
30	#4	60	Come and Go With Me	90	Traumerai by Schumann

The solos in the book (starting on page 14) are recorded in split track. The solo part (your part) will be on the right channel and the guitar accompaniment will be on the left. To play alone with the accompaniment, turn your balance knob all the way to the left.

Online Audio & Video

Audio
www.melbay.com/99931BCDEB
Video
dv.melbay.com/99931
You Tube
www.melbay.com/99931V

It doesn't get any easier.....

2 3 4 5 6 7 8 9 0

Visit us on the Web at www.melbay.com — E-mail us at email@melbay.com

Holding the Guitar

Position the guitar so that you are comfortable. The right hand should rest over the sound hole. The left hand should be able to reach the first fret.

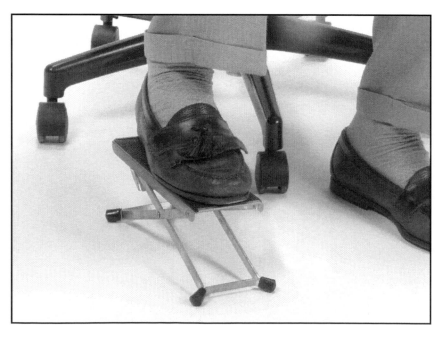

A footstool can be purchased at your local music store. The footstool is adjustable and can help elevate the guitar to a comfortable height.

Placing the Left Hand on the Guitar

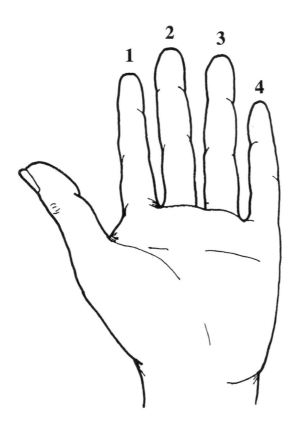

Left Hand Position

Place your fingers firmly on the strings directly behind the frets. The thumb should be placed in the center of the back of the neck. Do not wrap your thumb around the neck.

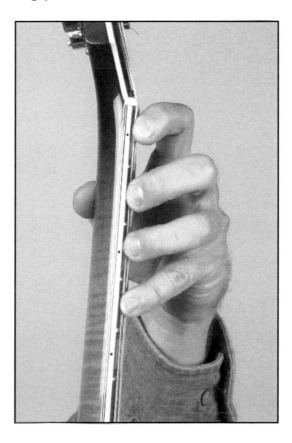

Holding the Pick

Flatpicks

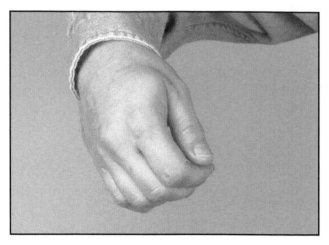

The right hand fingers are curved.
Keep the hand loose–not rigid.

The pick rests gently on the index finger with
the "point" aiming away from the thumb.

The thumb rests on top of the
pick to hold it in place.

■ = Downstroke of the pick.

Parts of the Guitar

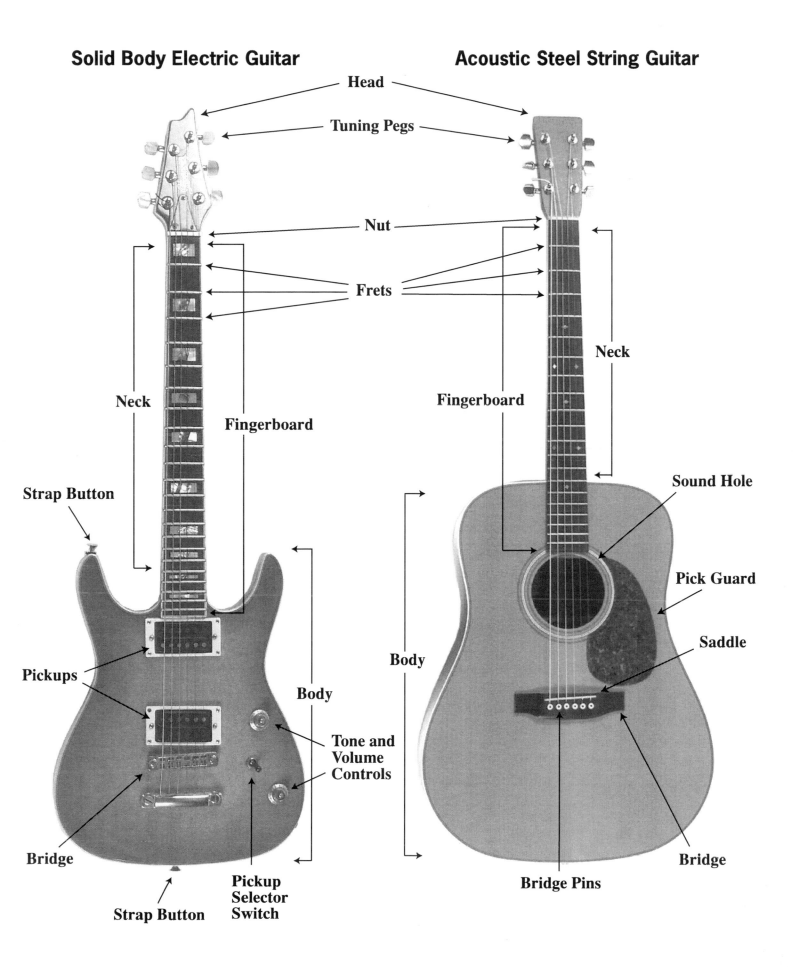

Solid Body Electric Guitar

Acoustic Steel String Guitar

Head

Tuning Pegs

Nut

Frets

Neck

Fingerboard

Neck

Fingerboard

Sound Hole

Strap Button

Pick Guard

Saddle

Body

Pickups

Body

Bridge

Tone and Volume Controls

Bridge

Strap Button

Pickup Selector Switch

Bridge Pins

Tuning the Guitar

6th   1st
5th   2nd
4th   3rd

 Listen to track #2 of your CD and tune up as follows!

1st String – E

2nd String – B

3rd String – G

4th String – D

5th String – A

6th String – Low E

Electronic Guitar Tuner

Electronic Guitar Tuners are available at your music store. They are a handy device and highly recommended.

6

Counting

We will use the following **Time Signatures**.

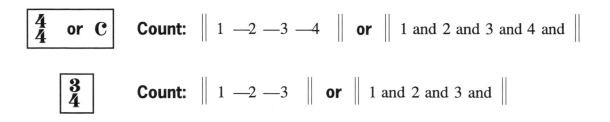

$\frac{4}{4}$ or **C**   **Count:** ‖ 1 —2 —3 —4 ‖ **or** ‖ 1 and 2 and 3 and 4 and ‖

$\frac{3}{4}$ **Count:** ‖ 1 —2 —3 ‖ **or** ‖ 1 and 2 and 3 and ‖

Types of Notes

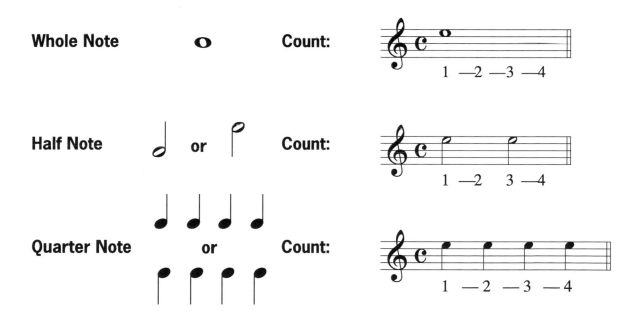

Whole Note   o   **Count:**   1 —2 —3 —4

Half Note   ♩ or ♩   **Count:**   1 —2   3 —4

Quarter Note   or   **Count:**   1 — 2 — 3 — 4

7

Notes on the High E String

First String

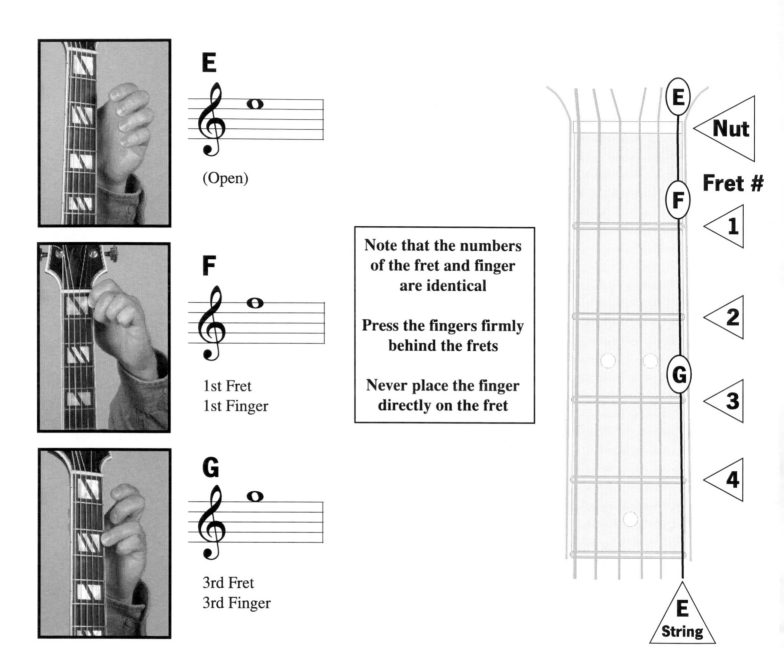

E

(Open)

F

1st Fret
1st Finger

G

3rd Fret
3rd Finger

Note that the numbers
of the fret and finger
are identical

Press the fingers firmly
behind the frets

Never place the finger
directly on the fret

Nut

Fret #

1

2

3

4

E
String

Playing the Notes

Notes on the B String

Second String

B

(Open)

C

1st Fret
1st Finger

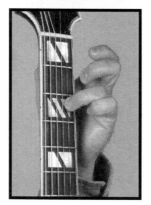

D

3rd Fret
3rd Finger

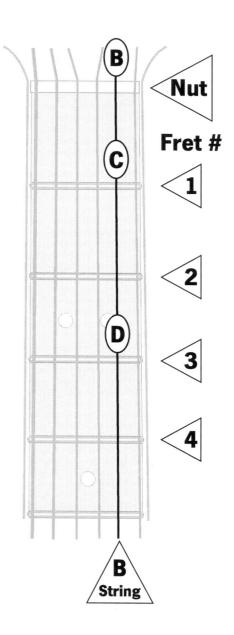

Playing the Notes

Playing on 2 Strings

3/4 Time

Count: | 1 - 2 - 3 | 1 - 2 - 3

1 💿 27

Count: 1 - 2 - 3

2 💿 28

Count: 1 - 2 3

Dotted Half Note

Receives
3 counts

Count: 1 - 2 - 3

3 💿 29

Count: 1 - 2 - 3

4 💿 30

Count: 1 - 2 - 3 - 4

5 💿 31

Count: 1 - 2 - 3 - 4

6 💿 32

Count: 1 - 2 3 - 4

7 💿 33

Count: 1 - 2 - 3 - 4

13

Notes on the G String

Third String

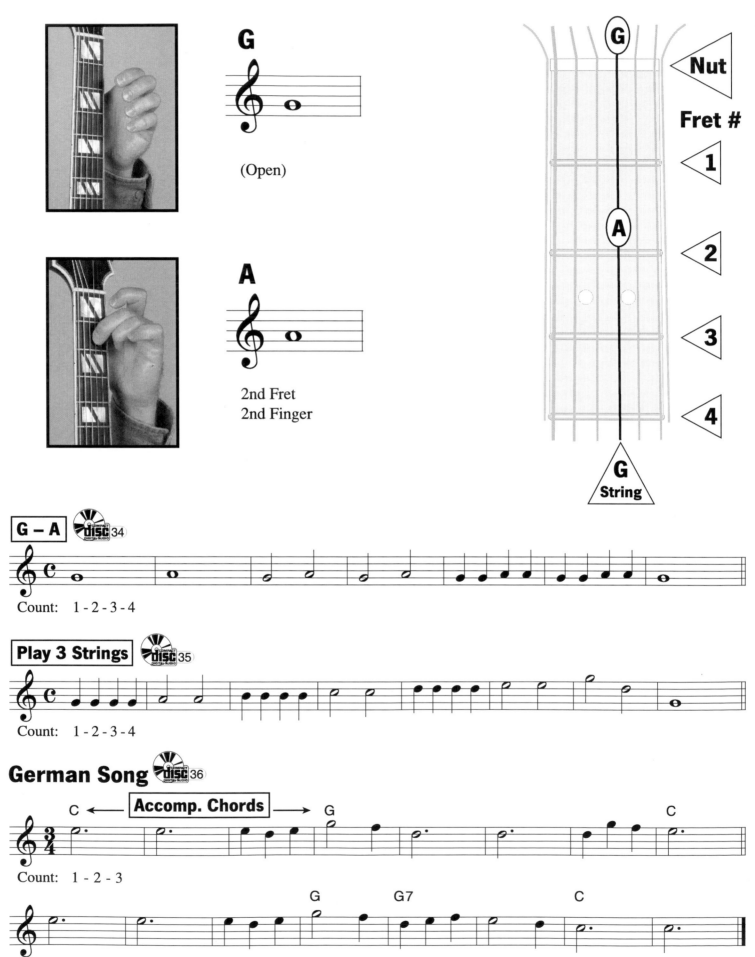

G
(Open)

A
2nd Fret
2nd Finger

Nut
Fret #
1
2
3
4
G String

G – A 34
Count: 1 - 2 - 3 - 4

Play 3 Strings 35
Count: 1 - 2 - 3 - 4

German Song 36
C ← **Accomp. Chords** → G   C
Count: 1 - 2 - 3

G   G7   C

Rock Feeling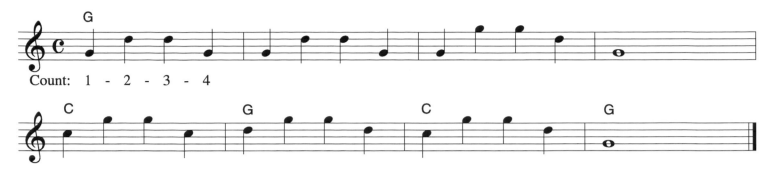

Count: 1 - 2 - 3 - 4

Indian Prayer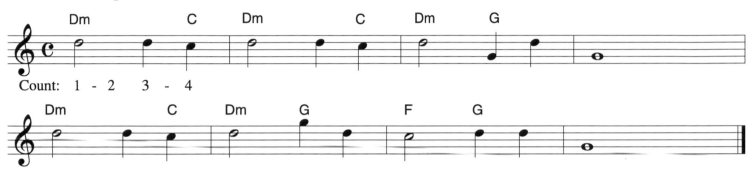

Count: 1 - 2   3 - 4

Good King Wenceslas

Count: 1 - 2 - 3 - 4

African Hymn

Count: 1 - 2   3 - 4

15

Rests

When a rest occurs, we count but do not play

Rest Study 💿41

Count: 1 - 2 - 3 - 4   1 - 2 - 3 - 4   1 - 2 - 3 - 4   1 - 2 - 3 - 4   1 - 2 - 3 - 4   1 - 2 - 3 - 4   1 - 2 - 3 - 4

I Know Where I'm Going 💿42

Count: 1 - 2 - 3 - 4   1 - 2 - 3 - 4

The Eighth Note

An eighth note receives one-half beat (one quarter note equals two eighth notes.)
An eighth note will have a head, stem, and flag. If two or more are in successive order, they may be connected by a bar. (See example.)

Eighth Notes   **Eighth Rests**

💿43

Count: 1 - 2 - 3 - 4   1 - 2   3 - 4   1 - 2 - 3 - 4   1 - 2 - 3 - 4 -   1 - 2 - 3 - 4

Count: 1 - 2   3 - 4 -

Count: 1 - 2 - 3 - 4 -

Count: 1 - 2 - 3 - 4

16

The Tie

A tie is a curved line that joins two or more notes of the same pitch. When you see a tie, only pick the first note.

Railroad Bill

Count: 1 - 2 - 3 - 4

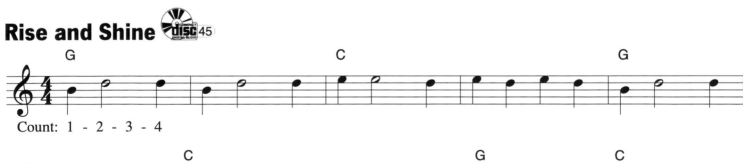

Rise and Shine

Count: 1 - 2 - 3 - 4

Notes on the D String

Fourth String

D

(Open)

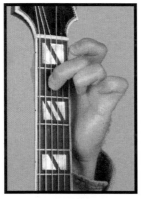

E

2nd Fret
2nd Finger

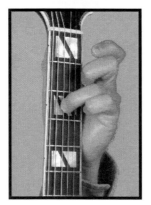

F

3rd Fret
3rd Finger

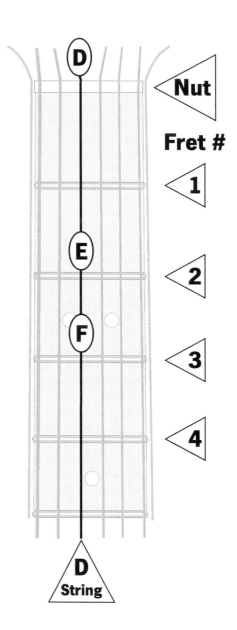

D String Notes

Picking Tunes

Down Shift

What's Up?

Nascar

19

Pick-Up Notes

Some songs start with less than a full 4 beat measure. These starting notes are called a "Pick-up."

Taps 🔘52

Count: 4   &   1 - 2 - 3   4   &

Reville 🔘53

Count: 4   1 - 2 & 3 - 4

Lonesome Valley 🔘54

G   C   Em   D

Count: 3   4   1 - 2 - 3 - 4   1 - 2 - 3 - 4

G   Bm   G   Em

C   D   C   G

Dotted Quarter Notes

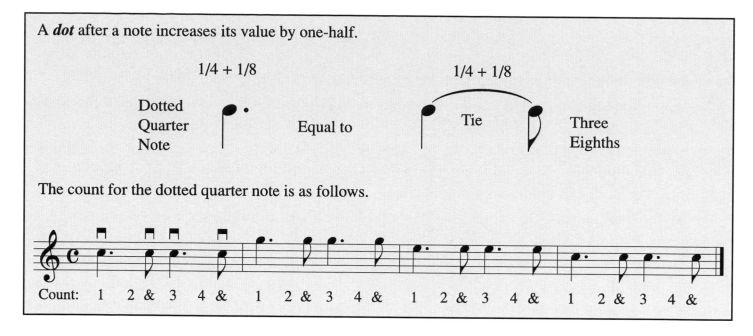

A *dot* after a note increases its value by one-half.

The count for the dotted quarter note is as follows.

Our Boys Will Shine Tonight

The Roving Gambler

More Solos

This Little Light of Mine

Count: 1 2 & 3 4

Precious Memories

Slowly

Count: 1 & 2 & 3 & 4 &

Early American Hymn

Count: 4 1 2 3 & 4 &

22

Come and Go with Me

Count: 3 & 4   1 2 3 4

Salty Dog Blues

Count: 2 3 4   1 2 & 3 4 &

Steal Away

Notes on the A String

Fifth String

A

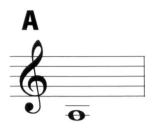

(Open)

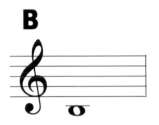

B

2nd Fret
2nd Finger

C

3rd Fret
3rd Finger

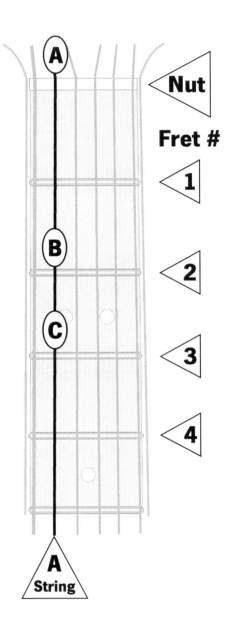

Notes on the Low E String

Sixth String

E

(Open)

F

1st Fret
1st Finger

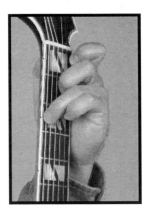

G

3rd Fret
3rd Finger

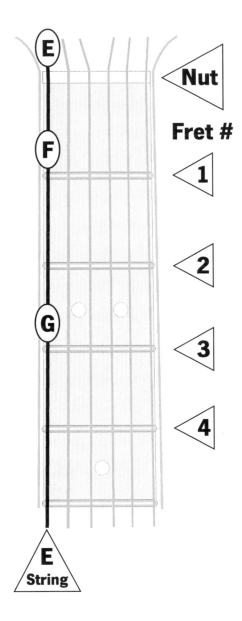

E String Notes

2

Note Review

Angelina the Baker

The Water Is Wide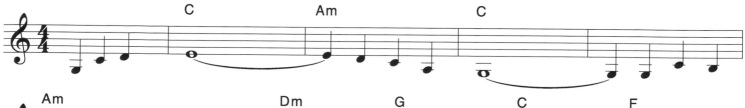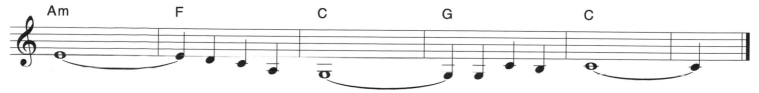

F♯

A *Sharp* (♯) sign before a note raises the note 1 fret. A *Natural* (♮) sign before a note brings it back to its normal pitch.

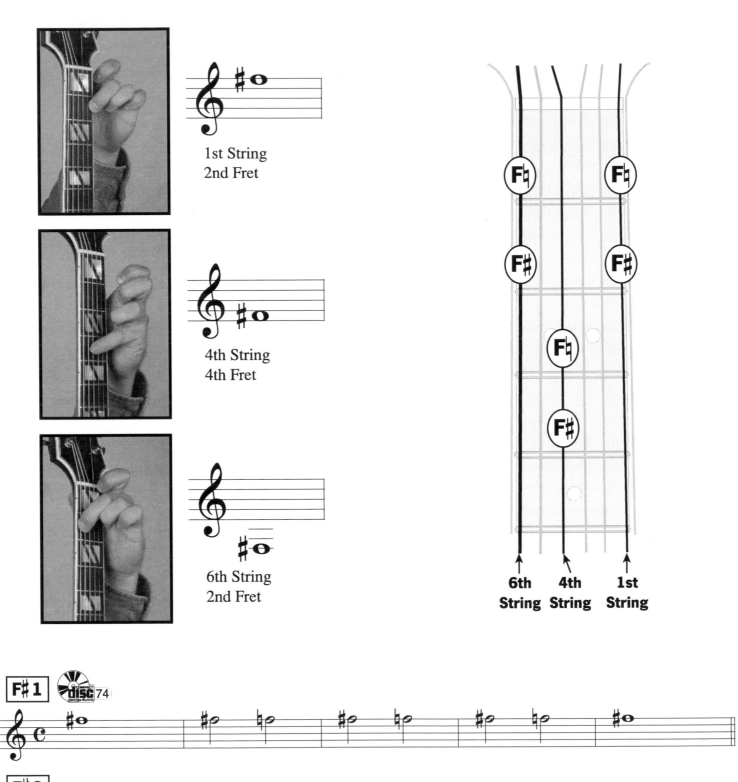

1st String
2nd Fret

4th String
4th Fret

6th String
2nd Fret

6th String   4th String   1st String

F♯1

F♯2

F♯3

Key Signature

When a sharp appears in the key signature, all notes of that pitch are sharped unless cancelled by a natural sign (♮).

Can Can 🔘disc 75

Polovetsian Dance 🔘disc 76

Hey, Ho, Nobody's Home 🔘disc 77

Eighth Rest (𝄾)

Receives the same time value as an eighth note.

I'm Gonna Play 🔘disc 78

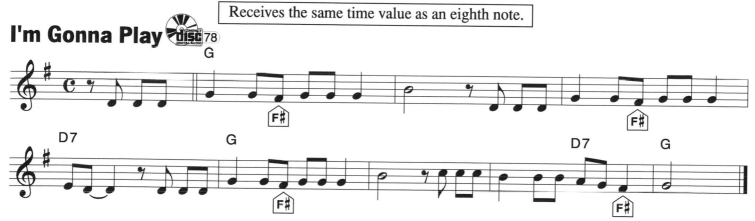

29

More Solos

Remember — if F# is in the key signature, all F's will be sharped unless a natural sign (♮) is in front of the F.

Matty Groves

Minuet by Bach

Waltzing Matilda

Introducing the A Note

A

5th Fret
4th Finger

Auld Lang Syne

Finlandia Theme

31

B♭

A *Flat* (♭) in front of a note lowers it by one fret. A flat is cancelled by a *Natural* (♮) sign. A flat in the key signature means that all notes of that pitch are flatted unless cancelled by a natural sign.

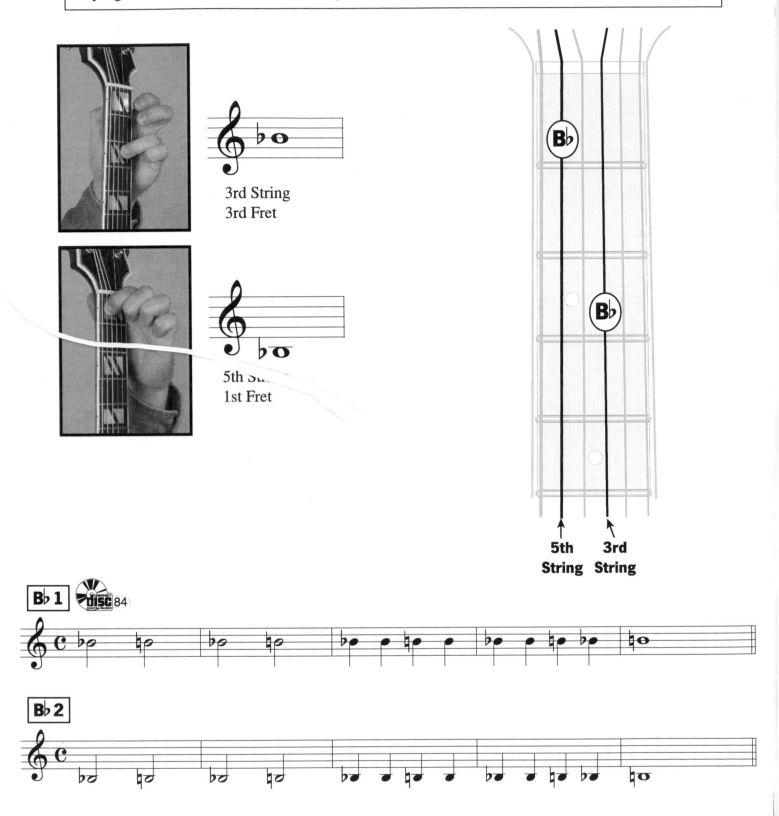

3rd String
3rd Fret

5th String
1st Fret

5th String   3rd String

B♭ 1

B♭ 2

Repeat Signs

Means to go back and repeat the phrase.

Forest Green

Red Wing

Once in David's Royal City

More Solos

Watch the key signature for B♭s!

Waltz by Chopin

Ding, Dong, Merrily on High

Traumerai by Schumann

Musical Terms

Tempo Terms

Largo	Very Slowly
Lento	Slowly
Adagio	Slowly with a very expressive feeling
Andante	A walking speed, however not too fast
Moderato	Moderately, medium speed
Allegretto	Slightly more movement than Moderato
Allegro	Quickly, lively tempo, but not overly fast or "out of control"
Vivaci	Very fast
Rit. "Ritardando"	Slow down at a gradual rate
Acc. "Accelerando"	Accelerate or speed up at a gradual rate

Dynamics

pp	(pianissimo)	Very soft
p	(piano)	Soft
mp	(mezzo piano)	Medium soft
mf	(mezzo forte)	Medium loud
f	(forte)	Loud
ff	(fortissimo)	Very loud
<	(crescendo)	Gradually get louder
>	(decresendo)	Gradually get softer
>	(accent)	The note is to be played louder

Phrasing Terms

8va	Play the passage 8th notes or one octave higher
Staccato	Play the notes so marked in a short detached manner
Legato	Play the notes so marked in a such as a tick or pluck the note so marked in a gentle somewhat connected manner. Almost as if the notes are slurred.
Rubato	Very expressive, no set tempo, notes may be played longer or shorter than their exact value in order to add expression.
ad lib	Playing at liberty, playing in a totally free fashion, improvising or making up a melody if a given section is marked so in a piece.

How to String a Guitar

Be sure to loosen each old string before cutting and removing from the guitar.

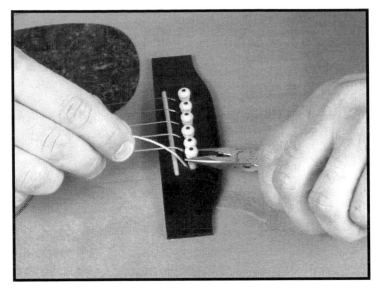

① Place ball end of string in bridge hole and replace bridge pin.

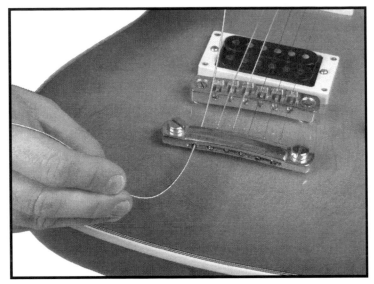

① With an electric guitar slide string through the appropriate tailpiece slot.

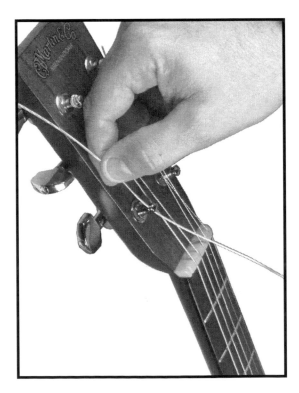

② Thread string through appropriate string peg hole.

③ Bend excess string back towards middle of guitar neck.

④ Pull excess string up and back so that, when you tighten the string by turning the tuning peg, the tightened string will "lock" the excess string in place.

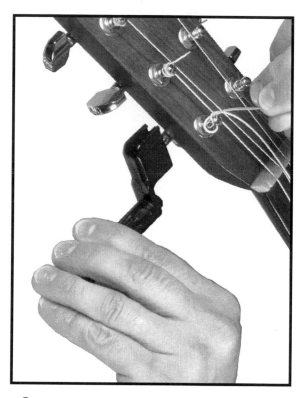

⑤ Tighten string and bring up to pitch. A plastic string winder (shown here) can be purchased at a music store.

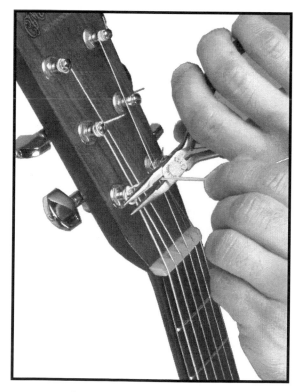

⑥ Cut off excess string.

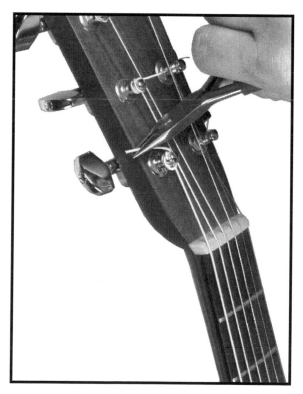

⑦ Bend stub back and out of the way.

For more detailed information on stringing all types of guitars, see Mel Bay's *Stringing the Guitar Chart* (MB99617).

Types of Guitars

Acoustic Steel String Guitar
Acoustic Steel String Guitars come in a variety of shapes and sizes. They have a round hole and give a clear, resonant sound. Usually, the larger the body, the deeper and richer the sound. Some are cut away for ease of fingering in higher positions. Bronze strings are usually played on these models. Some have an electric pickup and can be amplified.

Classic Guitar
Made with light, responsive woods and strung with nylon strings. Gives a mellow, rich tone. Does not project as loud a volume as a steel string acoustic. Some classics do come with a pickup and can be played through an amplifier. Used normally for classical and some fingerstyle performance.

Solid Body Electric
Must be played through an amplifier to gain volume. Has steel strings and is used in rock and blues music. Very easy to finger and can easily be played in very high positions. Usually very durable guitars since the body is a solid block of wood and since the sound is generated by the electronic pickups.

Hollow Body Electric
Usually has steel strings and a rather thin body. Gives a slightly more mellow electric sound than the solid body electric. Used often in blues and jazz. Can have nylon strings. (The model pictured has nylon). Gives an audible acoustic sound but needs amplification to be heard in a large room.

Arch Top Electric
The rich sounding model found in jazz music. Arch tops can be very costly if hand made but lower priced models made out of laminates are available and are frequently used. Sounds good acoustically or with amplification. Steel strings are used. Often flat wound or flat polished strings are played on this kind of guitar.

12 String Guitar
An acoustic steel string with 12 strings. Gives a rich, harp like sound and can be difficult to finger due to the doubling of the strings. Bronze strings are normally used on a 12 string acoustic model, Not recommended as a beginner's guitar.

Frequently Asked Questions

1. **Where should I go to find a good guitar? (Friends, online, pawnshops, etc.)**
A. Go to a music store that carries a full line of guitars and which will let you rent a good quality beginner's guitar. Ask about service. Do they repair guitars they sell?

2. **Should I buy or rent a guitar?**
A. Best bet is to rent a guitar when you start, provided that the rent paid will apply later on a purchase of any new or used guitar.

3. **What kind of guitar should I use when starting?**
A. Our advice is to start on an acoustic guitar, not an electric. Here is why. When starting, you need to learn to develop a good tone and you also need to develop good left hand technique. An electric will not give you the flexibility in developing a good acoustic tone. Also, some electrics have such low action or ease of fingering that you may be starting on an instrument with fingering too easy. (For example, how much good would you get by doing a "push up" if you only had to go 1/2 way up?)

4. **Should I start with nylon or steel string?**
A. Either will work, however, we do prefer nylon for young children provided that the guitar is of a suitably small size. Nylon strings are easier to finger for the beginner. You generally have less finger soreness during the first few weeks. If you do start on a steel string guitar make sure to use light gauge or extra light gauge strings. They will be easier to press down.

5. **What size should the guitar be?**
A. As a general rule the guitar should be small enough so that you can comfortably reach the first fret with the left hand and also easily reach down to strum the strings with the right hand. Size is very important. Never start with an oversized, jumbo guitar. Very fine 3/4 and 1/2 size guitars are now available for children and small adults. Do look into these smaller sizes when beginning.

6. **How young can someone start?**
A. This is changing because very fine guitars are now being made in small sizes for the young beginner and methods are being written with the small child in mind. As a general rule, I would say 5 is a very workable age to consider beginning guitar instruction (but there are some fine young students at age 4!)

7. **What if I am left handed?**
A. Generally, we have advised the left-handed student to play the guitar just like a right-handed student. The left handed student will then be fingering the instrument with his or her most nimble hand. There are guitars with the strings "reversed" and we do have books out for the left handed student who wants to finger with the right hand and strum with the left.

8. **Should I start with a pick or my fingers?**
A. We recommend starting to strum chords and notes with the right hand thumb. Then, move into using the flatpick unless you want to play classical or fingerstyle guitar.

9. **What if my fingers are sore?**
A. It is quite normal for the fingertips of the left (or fingering) hand to be tender or sore at the beginning . You will develop calluses after several weeks. Make sure you are using light or extra light gauge strings. If you are playing nylon strings and have continual sore fingers, try using a low tension string. Finally, make sure the strings are not too high off the fingerboard at the "nut". You can have this checked at your music store. This can easily be fixed by carefully filing down the string slots on the nut. This is a common adjustment needed for many student model guitars. Be sure, however, to have the music store do this for you.

10. **Should I use a strap when I play?**
A. A strap is used when standing and playing. Do not learn to play the guitar standing. Use proper seating posture shown earlier in this book.

11. **How often should I change the strings?**
A. The strings should be changed when they start to sound dull or when they become brittle to the fingers. For a beginner, this should not be more than once every three or four months

12. **Anything else I need to know about my guitar?**
A. The guitar is a wonderful instrument that can provide incredible fun and quality to your life. It will lead you into many styles and area of music if studied diligently. Take care of your instrument. Do not leave it in the sun or locked up in the car in extreme hot or cold temperatures. Avoid dropping it or placing it where it can fall.

13. **How long should I practice?**
A. Quality of practice is better than quantity, especially at the beginning. Thus, try to plan several 15 or 20 minute segments a day and work up from there. Never practice when you are tired and cannot concentrate on what you are doing.

Glossary of Guitar Terms

3/4-size guitar – A smaller than normal guitar with shorter strings and less space between frets.

action – A term referring to the height of the strings above the frets and fretboard.

altered and open tunings – The result of changing the tuning of one or more strings from standard EADGBE.

alternate picking – Picking in alternate directions (down-up-down-up).

arpeggio – A broken chord, usually played evenly low to high and back again.

arrangement – The setting of an original or standard tune for a given solo instrument or group of instruments

barre chord – From the French term *barré*. The technique of placing the left hand index finger over two to six strings in the fingering of a chord. The great advantage of using barre chords is that they are "moveable shapes" that can be applied at practically any fret.

bending – The act of pushing or pulling a string sideways across a fret to raise the pitch of a note by a half to full tone or more. Used extensivly in rock and blues playing as well as in jazz.

capo – a mechanical barre that attaches to the neck of a guitar by means of a string, spring, elastic or nylon band, or a lever and thumbscrew arrangement. The capo can be used to raise the key of a song to suit a vocalist as well as to lower the action and shorten the string length.

chord – Three or more notes sounded simultaneously.

chorus (of a tune) – Strictly speaking, the portion of a song lyric or melody that is repeated, often with other voices joining in. In jazz improvisation, however, "playing a chorus" would mean taking a turn improvising over the tune's chords progression.

closed voicing – The term "voicing" refers to the vertical arrangement of the notes of a given chord. "Closed voicing" places the member notes as close together as possible, no matter the inversion as opposed to "open voicing" which spreads the member notes as close together as possible, no matter the inversion as opposed to "open voicing" which spreads the member notes of the chord at larger intervals.

cutaway – A concave area generally in the upper right bout of a normal right-hand guitar that allows the player easier access to the high frets.

dropped-D tuning – The practice of lowering the sixth string (E) by a whole tone, one octave lower than the fourth string.

finger picks – Banjo-style picks that fingerstyle guitarists use when playing steel-string instruments.

fingerstyle – Playing with the fingernails or fingertips with or without fingerpicks as opposed to playing with a flatpick.

flatpick – A triangular or teardrop-shaped piece of nylon or plastic used to pluck or strum guitar strings. Flatpicks are available in a large variety of shapes, sizes, and thickness.

footstool – A small adjustable stool used to raise the height of the guitar.

hammer-on – A note sounded literally by "hammering" down with a left hand finger, often performed in conjunction with a note first plucked by the right hand on the same string.

harmonics – Chime-like sounds achieved in two ways:

    1) *natural harmonics* – by touching a string at any equidistant division of the string length (typically 5th, 7th, and 12th fret), directly above the fret with left hand, and striking hard with the right-hand fingers or pick near the bridge where there is more string resistance; or

    2) *artificial harmonics* – touching a string with the index finger of the right hand twelve frets higher than any fretted note and plucking the string with either the thumb or third finger of the right hand.

interval – The distance between two notes.

inversion – Structuring a chord with a note other than the root as the lowest note.

lead guitar – The part played by a guitar soloist in a rock band

modulate – To change keys within a piece of music

open voicing – A manner of chord construction in which the member notes are broadly separated. See *closed voicing* above.

pentatonic scale – A five-tone scale used often in rock.

picking – Plucking or producing a sound on the guitar in general, either with the fingers or a flatpick. Sometimes refers to playing a single-note melody line.

p i m a – letters derived from the Spanish names for the fingers of the right hand: *pulgar* (thumb), *indice* (index), *medio* (middle), and *anular* (ring). Used to indicate fingering.

plectrum – Another name for a flatpick.

positions – a reference to placement of the left hand index finger at various frets.

power chord – A chord consisting of the first (root), fifth and eighth degree (octave) of the scale. Power chords are typically used in playing rock music.

pull-off – The opposite of a hammer-on. Performed by plucking a note with a finger on a higher note and pulling parallel to the fret to sound a lower note on the same string.

rhythm guitar – Rhythmic strumming of chord backup for a lead player, singer, or ensemble.

setup – The adjustment of the action of a guitar for optimal playing characteristics.

slide – A plastic or glass tube placed over the third or fourth finger of the left hand and used to play "slide" or glissando effects in rock and blues and other forms of traditional music.

standard tuning – The guitar is generally tuned EADGBE low to high.

string winder – a swivel device with a handle with a fixture that fits over the tuning keys.

strumming – Performed with a pick or the fingers. Generally consists of brushing across 2-6 strings in a rhythmic up and down fashion appropriate to the tune being played.

tablature or tab – A system of writing music for fretted instruments whereby a number or letter appears on lines representing the strings, indicating the fret to be played.

transcription – To write a solo, note for note, off of a recording.

transpose – To change the key of a piece of music by a specific interval.

tremolo – a technique performed with either a very rapid down-up movement of the pick or a *pami* plucking of the fingers.

triad – A three-note chord.

tuner – An electronic tuning device.

vibrato – To vibrate by slightly altering a pitch higher and lower.

voicing – The arrangement of the member notes of a chord, or placement of the melody or bass line within a harmonic progression.